CONTENTS

A Welcome Letter......................
Core Expectations..6
Peace Corps/Moldova History and Programs...............................7
    History of the Peace Corps in Moldova...............................7
    History and Future of Peace Corps
    Programming in Moldova...7

Country Overview: Moldova at a Glance.....................................10
    History...10
    Government..11
    Economy..12
    People and Culture..13
    Environment...14

Resources for Further Information..14

General Information About Moldova...15

Living Conditions and Volunteer Lifestyle....................................18
    Communications...18
    Housing and Site Location..19
    Living Allowance and Money Management.......................20
    Food and Diet..21
    Transportation..22
    Geography and Climate...23
    Social Activities..23
    Professionalism, Dress, and Behavior................................24
    Personal Safety..25
    Rewards and Frustrations..26

Peace Corps Training..28
    Overview of Pre-Service Training......................................28
        Technical Training..29

    Language Training..29
    Cross-Cultural Training..30
    Health Training..30
    Safety Training..30
  Additional Trainings During Volunteer Service................................31

Your Health Care and Safety in Moldova...31
  Health Issues in Moldova..32
  Helping You Stay Healthy..32
  Maintaining Your Health..33
  Women's Health Information..33
  Your Peace Corps Medical Kit..34
  Before You Leave: A Medical Checklist..35
  Safety and Security—Our Partnership..37
    Factors that Contribute to Volunteer Risk..................................38
    Support from Staff...39
  Staying Safe: Don't Be a Target for Crime.......................................39
  Crime Data For Moldova..41
  Preparing for the Unexpected: Safety Training
  and Volunteer Support in Moldova...41

Diversity and Cross-Cultural Issues...42
  Overview of Diversity in Moldova..43
  What Might a Volunteer Face?..43
    Possible Issues for Female Volunteers......................................43
    Possible Issues for Volunteers of Color....................................44
    Possible Issues for Senior Volunteers.......................................45
    Possible Issues for Gay, Lesbian, or Bisexual Volunteers...........46
    Possible Religious Issues for Volunteers..................................47
    Possible Issues for Volunteers With Disabilities.......................48
    Possible Issues for Married Volunteers.....................................49

Frequently Asked Questions..49
Welcome Letters From Moldova Volunteers...54
Packing List..56
Pre-departure Checklist..59
Contacting Peace Corps Headquarters...62

PEACE CORPS/MOLDOVA HISTORY AND PROGRAMS

History of the Peace Corps in Moldova

In 1993, the government of Moldova invited Peace Corps to open a program in Moldova. The Peace Corps' first assignment was to help expand the English-teaching capacity of Moldovan educators. Government representatives believed that well-developed English language skills would help Moldovans participate in the international community and global economy by helping them gain access to a wealth of information, resources, and markets. Current English education Volunteers also incorporate environmental issues into the curriculum.

Recently, Peace Corps Moldova has added projects in community and organizational development, agribusiness and rural business development, and health education to assist the Moldovan government in addressing the country's economic and social development needs. Currently, Peace Corps Volunteers are working in about 100 towns and villages throughout the country. Since the program's inception, almost 1,000 Volunteers have served in Moldova.

History and Future of Peace Corps Programming in Moldova

Peace Corps Moldova works in four major project areas: English education, health education, community and organizational development, and agribusiness and rural business development. Project plans are jointly developed by Peace Corps staff, Volunteers, and Moldovan partners.

Peace Corps Volunteers (PCVs) assigned to the English Education (EE) project work at three levels: with students, teachers, and schools. They work as full-time, regular classroom teachers of English and teach in compliance with the requirements of the Moldovan National English Teaching Curriculum. EE Volunteers teach the majority of their classes alongside Moldovan teachers. This team teaching practice is designed to improve Moldovan teachers English language skills and to allow the Volunteer and Moldovan teacher to learn from each other and present high-quality lessons to students. Working both inside and outside of the classroom, PCVs and their teaching partners help students to improve their English language, critical thinking, problem solving, and decision making skills. They also seek to broaden students awareness of issues affecting their local communities, Moldova and the rest of the world. Working directly with their teaching colleagues, PCVs occassionaly implement training workshops and present model lessons designed to introduce teachers to different teaching practices. At the institutional level, PCVs work with their schools and communities to improve the quality and the quantity of resource materials available for teaching and learning English, promote the use of technology in education, improve community development, and promote community and parent involvement in schools.

During the Soviet era, the healthcare system in what is now the Republic of Moldova focused on curative and clinical care provided by the state as opposed to health promotion and disease prevention. In 1995, health education was introduced as an optional course in the Moldovan school system.

Education in basic life skills forms the framework for all health education conducted by the Peace Corps in Moldova. Volunteers are assigned jointly to secondary schools and local medical units or health-related, non-governmental organizations (NGOs).

Volunteer accomplishments have included assisting teachers to develop long-term plans and lesson plans for Health Education classes and youth clubs, assisting community health staff to develop and conduct health education activities for the adult population, developing materials for health education activities, and facilitating health campaigns and community health projects. Additionally, Volunteers have assisted in the development of youth-oriented health centers and health education resource centers. They have also worked to develop and distribute educational materials in Romanian *(the country's official language)* on reproductive health, HIV/AIDS, STIs, breast cancer prevention, and the dangers of the substance abuse.

The Community and Organizational Development (COD) project assigns Volunteers to work with local NGOs and municipal offices. These organizations are often seeking greater institutional capacity while struggling with the difficulties of poor internal financing, limited community outreach abilities, and overworked and overextended members of the organization. Volunteers in this project have worked alongside their Moldovan partners in the promotion of women's and children's rights, minority rights issues, youth development, senior citizen care, development of arts, environmental awareness, and general community development.

Volunteers in the Agribusiness and Rural Business Development (ARBD) project collaborate with local organizations that provide services in the area of information dissemination, consulting, training, and extension in agriculture, micro-credit institutions and saving and credit associations, and community economic development organizations. Partner organizations include locally registered NGOs working to become self-sufficient and self-sustainable business training institutes and municipal government offices. Volunteers are involved in a range of activities targeting organizational development (needs assessments, training skills, extension methodology, organizational management, customer services, transparency, and representation) and directly assist small businesses and private farmer clients of these organizations through strengthening production knowledge, training in financial management and business planning, and assisting in development of marketing skills and ideas.

While remaining focused on their primary activities as outlined in each project plan, Volunteers in all four projects engage in a wide variety of secondary activities. Volunteers have been involved in English clubs, development of a Moldovan branch of the Special Olympics, organizing self-esteem and leadership weekends, development of summer camps for youth with a focus on gender and development, sports, life skills, and business education, youth entrepreneurship programs, training peer education groups, conducting health education activities in kindergartens and promoting non-violence in the family. They have also helped their assigned communities obtain small grants for the renovation of school gymnasiums, school kitchens, dormitories at orphanages, the establishment of libraries and resource centers, the construction of greenhouses for winter farming, and the provision of heating for rural schools.

The Peace Corps is committed to working alongside its Moldovan partners in meeting the country's economic and social development challenges. Peace Corps Moldova will continue its emphasis on placing Volunteers in towns and rural villages, where the need is greater than in Chisinau and other large cities.

COUNTRY OVERVIEW: MOLDOVA AT A GLANCE

History

Moldova is uniquely located at the frontier of Eastern and Western cultures. This has contributed to a long and difficult struggle by the indigenous Moldovan people to maintain their cultural and political sovereignty. During the Middle Ages (as in modern times) Moldova, like other principalities in the region, engaged in efforts toward the maintenance and recognition of its independence, the defense of its territory, and the preservation of its borders.

One of the country's most glorious eras occurred during the reign of Stefan cel Mare (Steven the Great) between 1457 and 1504. During these years, Moldovans won impressive victories over the Turks, Tartars, Hungarians, Poles, and other invaders. This temporary success, however, was no guarantee of the nation's future stability. Under the permanent threat of invasion, the principalities of this region unified as a means to resist aggression. The first unification—of Transylvania, Moldova, and Muntenia—took place during the rule of Mihai Viteazul (1593 to 1601). Although short-lived, this event served as a precedent for the union of the principalities of Tara Romaneasca and Moldova to form a new country, Romania, in 1859.

Following the Crimean War, political stability in the area was fleeting. In 1856, Russia lost the southern region of Basarabia to Moldova, only to gain it back from Romania in 1878 at the Congress of Berlin. With the collapse of the Russian Empire in 1918, this area, made up of part of the present territory of Moldova and part of Ukraine, declared its independence and reunited with Romania. The newly formed Union of Soviet Socialist Republics refused to recognize this reunification, however, and in 1924 created the Moldavian Autonomous Soviet Socialist Republic. In June 1940, after Hitler and Stalin signed the 1939 Molotov-Ribbentrop pact of nonaggression, the Soviet Union annexed additional territory to form the Moldavian Soviet Socialist Republic (MSSR). In the early 1940s, as World War II raged in Europe, Romania again claimed the territory of the MSSR. As the war came to a conclusion, the Soviet Union annexed the region again for a final time.

Subsequently, in an attempt to create a uniform culture among the Soviet republics, the leadership of the Soviet Union began a period of intense Russification, replacing Moldovans' traditional Latin alphabet with the Cyrillic alphabet and Romanian with Russian as the official language.

The tone of Soviet leadership changed in 1986 with the introduction of a policy of *glasnost* (openness) by President Mikhail Gorbachev. This new policy permitted the pursuit of traditional culture by the Moldovan population and leadership and set the stage for the republic's independence. On August 27, 1991, Moldova declared its independence, an event that is now celebrated every year on that date. To restore the cultural heritage of the majority of its citizens, the Moldovan government reestablished Romanian, using the Latin alphabet, as the national language.

Government

In the early 1990s, the government was distracted and weakened by a proclamation of secession by ethnic Russians and ethnic Ukrainians in the Dniester region (primarily on the left or Eastern bank of the Nistru River) and Gagauzia in the southeast. The Moldovan government announced the declarations invalid and armed conflict ensued in the Transnistria area. The fighting stopped in 1992, but a final settlement for Transnistria is still under negotiation, with both sides officially committed to a peaceful resolution. The conflict with Gagauzia has been resolved through elections and the establishment of the semiautonomous region of Gagauzia.

The first multiparty presidential elections were held in the fall of 1996 and were generally regarded as fair. The winner, Petru Lucinschi, assumed office in January 1997. Since July 2000, the president has been elected by Parliament for a four-year term under a parliamentary system modeled on the system in Italy. The parliamentary elections held in 2001 as well as in 2005 were won by the Party of Communists.

In April 2009, new elections were held, which the Party of Communists won. These results were initially hotly contested and a large protest in Chisinau turned into rioting within a few days of the vote. The Moldovan constitution has a unique requirement for 3/5ths majority of parliament to elect a President or else call for new elections. The Parliament elected in April 2009, having twice failed to elect a President was disbanded and new elections were held in July. This election was won by a group of parties (now called the Alliance for European Integration) opposed to the Party of Communists. This Alliance, holding an even smaller majority than the Party of Communists, also failed to elect a President. As the Moldovan constitution only allows two parliamentary elections in a given year, the country is currently governed by the Alliance for European Integration and an Acting President. . New elections were held in November 2010 and the same each of 3/5 as majority occurred. Currently the Temporary government has Marian Lupu as President and Vladimir Filat as prime minister.

Economy

With fertile soils and bountiful sunshine during the growing season, the Republic of Moldova is primarily an agrarian country. Because of its plentiful natural resources, Soviet Moldova was assigned the role of supplier of foodstuffs for the rest of the Soviet Union. More than half of its population still lives in rural areas, and approximately 40 percent of the workforce is engaged in horticulture, viticulture, or animal husbandry. The agricultural sector accounts for about 11 percent (World Bank 2008) of the gross domestic product. If agribusiness is included, the degree of dependence on agriculture becomes even greater, as food processing contributes approximately 40 percent to the country's industrial production. Jointly, these sectors constitute a third of the GDP and more than half of all merchandise exports.

Other industries, while never as significant as agribusiness, tend to be concentrated in Transnistria and therefore suffered disproportionately during the civil war in 1992. This is particularly true for heavy industries such as machinery. Consequently, the proportion of employment and output accounted for by industry is low, and most industrial companies still have underutilized capacities.

Disparities remain between the economic development of urban and rural areas. In 2008, 22 percent of Moldova's economic output came from direct agricultural production, based and 18 percent was based on manufacturing industries, almost half of which was related to agriculture. The remainder is attributed to the service sectors. After the recession of the 1990s, which cut GDP to almost a third of its pre-independence level, the Moldovan economy experienced strong and steady growth until it began to suffer from the current global financail crisis. The growth during this period was largely driven by the stability of the Russian economy, high consumption fueled by remittances from Moldovans working abroad; and low inflation. Even during this period of growth, though, Moldova's economy was intermittantly impacted by Russian economic policy and political relatiosn including a ban on imports of Moldovan wine and agricultural products combined with higher tariffs on natural gas imports- Moldova is totally dependent on Russia for gas and primarily dependant upon Ukraine for electricity.

Moldova's annual per capita GDP remains one of the lowest in Europe at U.S. $2,400 (2009).

People and Culture

Despite Moldova's small size, its population is quite diverse. According to the 2004 census, the majority of the population (78 percent) consists of Moldovans or people of Romanian descent. Other significant ethnic groups include Ukrainians (8 percent), Russians (6 percent), Gagauzians (4 percent), Bulgarians (2 percent), Roma (0.4 percent), and Jews (0.1 percent). Small numbers of Belorussians, Germans, Poles, and Turks also live in Moldova.

The official language of Moldova, as specified by the Constitution, is Moldovan (Romanian,) written in the Latin alphabet. Although Russian is no longer the official language, many Moldovans, especially in urban areas, are more familiar with Russian than with Romanian. Several years ago, the issue of declaring Russian as a second official language was the subject of great national debate and political demonstrations. As a Peace Corps Volunteer in Moldova, you will need to exercise a large degree of diplomacy when dealing with the language issue. Although certain regions or communities are predominantly Romanian or Russian speaking, there is considerable intermingling of the two, which can present linguistic challenges. You will also meet people who understand both languages but do not want to speak one or the other for personal or political reasons. English is spoken by increasing numbers of younger people, but fluency is still rare in most areas, and proficiency in Romanian or Russian is vital for Volunteers to be effective.

Moldovans are open, warm, friendly, and generous people and are renowned for their hospitality. However, living and working in a culture that is not your own can be frustrating and uncomfortable at times. As a guest in Moldova, you will be expected to respect the country's culture and traditions and make a host of adaptations to fit in. If you are willing to be open to all the good things that Moldova has to offer and to demonstrate understanding toward people undergoing difficult economic and political changes, you will be rewarded with one of the greatest experiences of your life.

Environment

Strategically located at the crossroads of central, southeastern, and Eastern Europe, the Republic of Moldova is the second smallest of the Newly Independent States. Situated along the Danube, Prut, and Nistru rivers, Moldova occupies 13,000 square miles and has a population of approximately 4.4 million. The country borders Romania in the west and Ukraine in the east and south. Its central region, the Basarabian Plateau, consists of forested highlands (up to 1,300 feet in elevation) and is known as the Codru. Most Volunteers easily adjust to Moldova's geographic environment.

RESOURCES FOR FURTHER INFORMATION

Following is a list of websites for additional information about the Peace Corps and Moldova and to connect you to returned Volunteers and other invitees. Please keep in mind that although we try to make sure all these links are active and current, we cannot guarantee it. If you do not have access to the Internet, visit your local library. Libraries offer free Internet usage and often let you print information to take home.

A note of caution: As you surf the Internet, be aware that you may find bulletin boards and chat rooms in which people are free to express opinions about the Peace Corps based on their own experience, including comments by those who were unhappy with their choice to serve in the Peace Corps. These opinions are not those of the Peace Corps or the U.S. government, and we hope you will keep in mind that no two people experience their service in the same way.

General Information About Moldova

www.countrywatch.com/
On this site, you can learn anything from what time it is in the Chisinau to how to convert from the dollar to the *leu*. Just click on Moldova and go from there.

www.lonelyplanet.com/destinations
Visit this site for general travel advice about almost any country in the world.

www.state.gov
The State Department's website issues background notes periodically about countries around the world. Find Moldova and learn more about its social and political history. You can also go to the site's international travel section to check on conditions that may affect your safety.

www.psr.keele.ac.uk/official.htm
This includes links to all the official sites for governments worldwide.

www.geography.about.com/library/maps/blindex.htm
This online world atlas includes maps and geographical information, and each country page contains links to other sites, such as the Library of Congress, that contain comprehensive historical, social, and political background.

www.cyberschoolbus.un.org/infonation/info.asp
This United Nations site allows you to search for statistical information for member states of the U.N.

www.worldinformation.com
This site provides an additional source of current and historical information about countries around the world.

Connect With Returned Volunteers and Other Invitees

www.rpcv.org
This is the site of the National Peace Corps Association, made up of returned Volunteers. On this site you can find links to all the Web pages of the "Friends of" groups for most countries of service, comprised of former

Volunteers who served in those countries. There are also regional groups that frequently get together for social events and local volunteer activities. Or go straight to the Friends of Moldova site: http://moldrpcv.tripod.com/.

http://www.rpcvwebring.org

This site is known as the returned Peace Corps Volunteer Web ring. Browse the Web ring and see what former Volunteers are saying about their service.

www.peacecorpswriters.org
This site is hosted by a group of returned Volunteer writers. It is a monthly online publication of essays and Volunteer accounts of their Peace Corps service.

Online Articles/Current News Sites About Moldova

http://lcweb2.loc.gov/frd/cs/mdtoc.html
A Library of Congress Federal Research Division study of Moldova

www.news.ournet.md
A Moldovan Web portal

www.ngo.md/index_eng.html
A listing of nongovernmental organizations in Moldova

International Development Sites About Moldova

www.unhcr.ch
Site of the United Nations High Commissioner for Refugees

www.info.usaid.gov/pubs/cp2000/eni/moldova.html
A Web page with information on the U.S. Agency for International Development's work in Moldova

Recommended Books

1. Kaplan, Robert D. Balkan Ghosts: A Journey Through History. NY: Picador: distributed by Holtzbrinck Publishers, 2005.

2. King, Charles. The Moldovans: Romania, Russia, and the Politics of Culture. Palo Alto, Calif.: Hoover Institution Press, 2000.

3. Kokker, Steve. Lonely Planet Romania and Moldova. Footscray, Victoria; London: Lonely Planet Publications, 2004.

3. Mitrasca, Marcel. Moldova: A Romanian Province Under Russian Rule : Diplomatic History from the Archives of the Great Powers. New York: Algora Publishing, 2002.

4. Smith, Hedrick. The New Russians (revised edition). New York: Random House, 1991. (Note: this book does not refer specifically to Moldova, but it does provide a good framework for examining issues in the former Soviet Union.)

Books About the History of the Peace Corps

1. Hoffman, Elizabeth Cobbs. *All You Need is Love: The Peace Corps and the Spirit of the 1960s*. Cambridge, Mass.: Harvard University Press, 2000.

2. Rice, Gerald T. *The Bold Experiment: JFK's Peace Corps*. Notre Dame, Ind.: University of Notre Dame Press, 1985.

3. Stossel, Scott. *Sarge: The Life and Times of Sargent Shriver*. Washington, D.C.: Smithsonian Institution Press, 2004.

Books on the Volunteer Experience

1. Dirlam, Sharon. *Beyond Siberia: Two Years in a Forgotten Place*. Santa Barbara, Calif.: McSeas Books, 2004.

2. Casebolt, Marjorie DeMoss. *Margarita: A Guatemalan Peace Corps Experience*. Gig Harbor, Wash.: Red Apple Publishing, 2000.

3. Erdman, Sarah. *Nine Hills to Nambonkaha: Two Years in the Heart of an African Village*. New York, N.Y.: Picador, 2003.

4. Hessler, Peter. *River Town: Two Years on the Yangtze*. New York, N.Y.: Perennial, 2001.

5. Kennedy, Geraldine ed. *From the Center of the Earth: Stories out of the Peace Corps*. Santa Monica, Calif.: Clover Park Press, 1991.

6. Thompsen, Moritz. *Living Poor: A Peace Corps Chronicle*. Seattle, Wash.: University of Washington Press, 1997 (reprint).

LIVING CONDITIONS AND VOLUNTEER LIFESTYLE

Communications

Mail

Mail service in Moldova is not completely reliable. Letters to and from Moldova typically arrive in two to three weeks, but some letters and flat mail never reach Volunteers. Advise family and friends not to send anything of value via flat mail. Packages generally arrive safely, although they are often opened by Customs agents and some contents are occasionally lost in transport. During pre-service training, letters should be sent to you at the following address:

"Your Name," PCT
Corpul Pacii
Str. Grigore Ureche 12
2001 Chisinau
Republica Moldova

Packages sent to Moldova by airmail arrive as quickly as letters but can be quite expensive, costing as much as $10 per pound. During pre-service training, packages can be sent to the same address as letters. Once you move to your site, you can make arrangements to receive mail and packages there, or continue to receive mail at the Peace Corps Office.

Telephones

Communication by telephone, both domestically and internationally, is more complicated in Moldova than in the United States, but is still manageable. There are a number of ways to call the United States, but the cost can be high. American calling cards will not work in Moldova, but international phone cards can be purchased that will give you enough time to give your family your phone number and instructions on when to call you back. Normal calls to the U.S. can cost about 50 cents per minute; phone cards can be purchased that will cost about 15-20 cents per minute; phone calls via computers (Skype, etc.) can cost about 2 cents per minute or be free for PC to PC calls (not including the cost of connecting to the Internet).

Your home will have a phone, and you will find that many people (Moldovans, Volunteers, and others) have cellphones. International lines are clearest early in the mornings and on weekends. Moldovan time is seven hours ahead of Eastern Standard Time.

Cellphones are not purchased for Volunteers by the Peace Corps. The cellular phone system in Moldova works on GSM technology. Unlocked GSM cell phone purchased in the United States will typically work here, but other cellular technologies will not.

Computer, Internet, and E-mail Access

The computerization of Moldova is progressing rapidly, so e-mail, blogs, Skype, and social networking sites are among the most common way Volunteers remain in contact with friends and family in the United States. If you have a laptop computer, you should consider bringing it, although Internet service in villages may be limited dial up or via the cellular phone network. On the other hand, many villages now have access to high speed Internet even in places where there is no gas or running water! Volunteers can access e-mail at the Peace Corps office, and the number of cybercafés around the country is growing.

Note that the Peace Corps does not provide any reimbursement for lost or stolen electronic equipment and cannot provide technical support or assistance with maintenance. Insurance against theft is a good idea.

Housing and Site Location

You will live with one host family during pre-service training (your first 8 to 10 weeks in country) and with another family for at least the first three months at your permanent site. You will have your own room, but you are likely to share kitchen, bath, and toilet facilities with the entire family. Houses seldom have indoor plumbing in most rural areas, so you may not have running water or an indoor toilet. After your first three months at site, you will have the option of finding other housing if it is available, meets Peace Corps' safety requirements, and can be leased within the Peace Corps' housing allowance. Most Volunteers choose to live with a family throughout their two years of service and find the experience a rewarding one.

Life in Chisinau, the capital, varies considerably from life in villages, where the pace is slower and the atmosphere is charmingly rustic. But, along with the great appeal of a gentler pace, villages in Moldova offer a somewhat arduous lifestyle. The primary form of entertainment is socializing with friends with modern forms of entertainment including watching television, listening to radio, surfing the Internet becoming more popular. People live the life of a farm family even if they work in a profession such as teaching. Each household usually has a very large vegetable garden and farm animals that they raise. There is generally no running water, outhouses are the most common toilet facilities, and bathing is usually done once a week in a bathhouse or using buckets of water in a tub. Despite the lack of amenities, however, life in a village will be rich in traditional Moldovan customs and friendships with Moldovans.

Towns or regional centers lack some of the compelling appeal of rural Moldova, and the pace is somewhat faster. There are more local resources, more forms of entertainment, and housing with running water is more common. Running water does not necessarily mean an indoor toilet, however, as the first priorities for plumbing are providing water for the kitchen and the garden.

Streets and sidewalks are muddy for a large part of the year in towns and villages alike. Heating in winter can be problematic, as many municipalities cannot afford to turn on the heat until long after the weather has turned cold, and ,even then, heating may be minimal or nonexistent for periods of time. For this reason, host families are required to have independent heating sources. Most families in villages rely on ceramic stoves, called *sobas*, that are built into the walls and burn wood, coal, or corncobs. In larger towns or cities, houses may have their own gas boiler.

Living Allowance and Money Management

After pre-service training, you will receive a monthly living allowance in local currency that will allow you to maintain your health and safety while living at a standard comparable to your Moldovan counterparts.

Moldova has a cash economy, and Moldovan banks and currency exchange offices are stringent about the condition of the U.S. banknotes they will accept due to concerns about counterfeit currency. Make sure that any U.S.

currency you bring is not worn, torn, or written on, and that the bills are fairly new. A few banks accept traveler's checks; others allow cash withdrawals via credit card or ATM card. There are increasing numbers of the machines in both Chisinau and regional centers, although Volunteers are advised to be cautious about which machines they use as ATM crimes are common. We discourage you from having cash sent to you from home, as sending money through international mail is risky. Furthermore, having your Peace Corps allowances substantially subsidized by funds from home runs counter to Peace Corps' philosophy of living at a similar level to those people with whom you work and serve.

In an emergency, you can have money sent through Western Union or international bank transfer. Most businesses, including restaurants and hotels, do not accept traveler's checks or credit cards. Those that do most commonly accept Visa. Some will charge you more for paying with a credit card.

If possible, we recommend that you keep an U.S. bank account with ATM capabilities to assist you with accessing occassional or emergency money from home. It will be the easiest way for Peace Corps to provide you with your Readjustment Allowance when you complete your Volunteer service, and is typically easier and quicker than having a check mailed to your U.S. home of record.

Once again, it is important to recognize that your Moldovan co-workers and friends will not have large sums of money or credit cards and that conspicuous displays of wealth on your part could drive a wedge between you and them. The Peace Corps discourages you from living beyond your monthly allowance.

Food and Diet

Moldovans love to cook, and they love their guests to eat a lot. Many traditional Moldovan dishes have roots in the Slavic and Romanian cultures. Pork is the meat of choice, followed by chicken, turkey, beef, and rabbit.

The national dish of Moldova is *mamaliga*, which is made from cornmeal and tastes somewhat like polenta or grits. It is served with soft cheese, meat, eggs, butter, or fish. Another interesting dish is *achituri*, which consists of chicken pieces in a brothlike jelly made of bone marrow and is usually served cold. *Coltsunashi*, which is similar to ravioli, is usually filled with potato, cheese, cabbage, and meat (or sometimes cherries) and served with butter or sour cream. *Friptura* is a beef or pork stew, sometimes baked with dough on top and usually served with vegetables. Similar to Greek dolmades, *sarmale* consists of grape leaves, green peppers, or cabbage stuffed with rice, meat, and vegetables. Moldovan barbecue is called *frigarui* or *shashlik*. *Borsh* is made with cabbage and other vegetables, and *chiorba* is made with meat, beans, and pasta. *Zeama* is a tasty chicken soup. *Placinta*, a baked or fried pastry, is filled with potato, cheese, cabbage, or fruit. Foods that should taste more familiar include *brinza* (a soft cow or sheep cheese), *cashcaval* (a hard, mild cheese), *smintina* (similar to sour cream), pilaf (rice with meat and vegetables), *clatite* (similar to crêpes), and *tocanista* (cooked vegetables).

Vegetarians may find it challenging to maintain their usual diet. It may also be difficult to explain why you are a vegetarian in a meat-and-potatoes culture. Although the concept of vegetarianism will not be entirely new to most Moldovans, you should expect some surprise and confusion. You will have to be clear about what you can and cannot eat (e.g., most soups have meat-based broths). You will also have to be sensitive and gracious when Moldovans try to prepare special food for you. If you offer to cook your own food, Moldovans will be curious to see how someone can actually prepare a dish with no meat. Yet many Moldovan dishes can easily be made without meat, so there is no reason why you cannot maintain a healthy vegetarian diet in Moldova. Vegans will have a more difficult time maintaining their diet and should consult the health unit in Moldova about maintaining a healthy vegan diet in Moldova .

Transportation

Operation of motor vehicles of any kind (e.g., cars, motor scooters, and motorcycles) is prohibited for Peace Corps Volunteers. Violation of this policy will result in termination of your service. Peace Corps policy also requires the use of a bicycle helmet, which the Peace Corps provides, when riding bicycles.

Volunteers will rely mostly on public transportation in Moldova. All the towns and villages in which Volunteers are placed have regularly scheduled bus or "maxi-taxi" service to Chisinau and other towns. In the case of an emergency, Peace Corps staff can get to any site by car within four hours.

Geography and Climate

The landscape of Moldova consists of hilly plains with an average altitude of about 150 meters (495 feet) above sea level, which flatten gradually toward the southwest. Old forests called *codrii* cover the central part of the country. Moldova is in an earthquake zone connected to the Carpathian Mountains. The last major earthquake occurred in 1989.

Moldova's two major rivers are the Nistru and the Prut, and a short span of the Danube crosses the extreme southern part of the republic. There are more than 3,000 small rivers or tributaries, of which only seven are longer than 50 miles. Moldova has more than 50 natural lakes and is rich in mineral-water springs.

The country has a temperate climate with four definite seasons; some Volunteers liken it to Minnesota. Summers are warm and humid, with an average high temperature in July of 80 degrees Fahrenheit; hot days in the 90s or even over 100 are not unusual. Winters are cold. Temperatures can remain below zero degrees Fahrenheit for weeks, and although snowfall is not extreme, it oftentimes remains in place for a month or more. Some offices and classrooms are poorly heated during the winter, requiring Volunteers to dress very warmly for work. Volunteers are also normally required to wear mutliple layers of clothing to remain warm at home during the winters. Spring and Autumn are usually beautiful with mild temperatures.

Social Activities

Chisinau, the capital, offers a wide variety of cultural and entertainment possibilities, such as opera, ballet, theater, circuses, and nightclubs (at which Moldovans love to dance). The options decrease, however, in proportion to the population of the community. In the smaller cities, there are cinemas, community centers, and universities at which plays, concerts, and other cultural events are occasionally presented. In villages, people socialize with relatives and friends, getting together in someone's home for fun and relaxation.

It is extremely important to develop a network of friends for social interaction, whether you live in a town or a village. Generally speaking, you should not expect to socialize with many single people of your own age. Moldovans tend to marry young and to stay married, so most adults are likely to be married and have children. Any single friends will probably be students.

Professionalism, Dress, and Behavior

One of the challenges of being a Peace Corps Volunteer is fitting into the local culture while maintaining your own cultural identity and acting as a professional all at the same time. It is not an easy situation to resolve, and we can only provide you with guidelines. As a member or representative of a school faculty, business development center, non-governmental organization, farmers' association, or health center, you will be expected to display sensitivity and respect toward your supervisor and colleagues in order to develop mutually-beneficial working relationships.

Moldovans are typically well educated and take pride in their education and abilities. Finding ways to demonstrate your own professional competence and willingness to work while simultaneously demonstrating a humble respect for the skills and abilities of your partners will be essential to your success. Inherent in Peace Corps' model is the understanding that better ideas and approaches result from people with different backgrounds working in partnership and learning alongside each other. While seldom easy, this is the only path toward long-term success as a Peace Corps Volunteer. Come prepared to put your patience, problem-solving, and communication skills to perhaps the greatest tests of your life.

As a rule, Moldovans pay attention to the way they dress. Dressing professionally and neatly is regarded as a sign of respect toward others and is important for gaining credibility with Moldovans. This cannot be overestimated. In general terms, Americans tend to dress casually and place more emphasis on what a person knows and what a person can do rather than on outward appearances. It can be difficult for Americans to understand the cultural significance of dressing appropriately and dressing well. Nonetheless, it is an expectation for Volunteers in Moldova to dress professionally when at the workplace. The more quickly you can adapt to this norm, the more easily you will integrate into your living and working communities in Moldova. Please plan the wardrobe you will bring with you accordingly. In order to help Trainees and Volunteers to get off to the best start possible with host families, neighbors, and future work partners, Peace Corps Moldova staff strongly recommend Volunteers to remove obvious and multiple facial piercings and cover highly visible tattoos to aid Volunteers to be accepted initially by host families, supervisors, partners, students, and neighbors. Please contact the country desk if you have any questions.

Teachers in Moldova tend to dress more formally than teachers do in the United States. Business casual (slacks, dress shirts, and dress shoes—preferably highly shined and black) is appropriate attire for men, whether working for a non-governmental organization or a school. Most women may wear professional-looking dresses or skirts and tops, but nice slacks are also acceptable in most places.

Another cultural issue is the role of alcohol in Moldovan society This can be a delicate issue as Volunteers will need to find a healthy balance between being an active participant in Moldovan culture while appropriately representing America and the Peace Corps. Many Moldovans make their own wine and spirits, and proudly encourage guests to try them. Being very good hosts, they will make sure that your glass is always full and will exert pressure on you to continue to drink. You will have to decide for yourself how much is appropriate for you and learn to politely and firmly refuse if you do not want to drink any more. While cultural sensitivity and social graces are important, it is more important that you know your limits and not endanger your health or your safety, or those of others.

Personal Safety

More detailed information about the Peace Corps' approach to safety is contained in the "Health Care and Safety" chapter, but it is an important issue and cannot be overemphasized. As stated in the *Volunteer Handbook,* becoming a Peace Corps Volunteer entails certain safety risks. Living and traveling in an unfamiliar environment (oftentimes alone), having a limited understanding of local language and culture, and being perceived as well-off are some of the factors that can put a Volunteer at risk. Many Volunteers experience varying degrees of unwanted attention and harassment. Petty thefts and burglaries are not uncommon, and incidents of physical and sexual assault do occur, although most Moldova Volunteers complete their two years of service without incident. The Peace Corps has established procedures and policies designed to help you reduce your risks and enhance your safety and security. These procedures and policies, in addition to safety training, will be provided once you arrive in Moldova. Using these tools, you are expected to take responsibility for your safety and well-being.

Each staff member at the Peace Corps is committed to providing Volunteers with the support they need to successfully meet the challenges they will face to have a safe, healthy, and productive service. We encourage Volunteers and families to look at our safety and security information on the Peace Corps website at www.peacecorps.gov/safety.

Information on these pages gives messages on Volunteer health and Volunteer safety. There is a section titled "Safety and Security in Depth." Among topics addressed are the risks of serving as a Volunteer, posts' safety support systems, and emergency planning and communications.

Rewards and Frustrations

Despite a few certain frustrations, Volunteer job satisfaction in Moldova is quite high. The pace of work and life is slower in most Moldovan communities than what most Americans are accustomed to, and some people you work with may be hesitant to alter long-held practices and traditions, including some stemming from the Soviet era. Different cultural concepts of timeliness and what constitutes a promise or pledge also confuse Volunteers leading to frustration. Most of these misunderstandings, with time, become more easily expected and better understood.

You will be given a high degree of responsibility and independence in your work—perhaps more than in any other job you have had or will ever have again. You will often find yourself in situations that require an ability to motivate both yourself as well as your counterparts with little guidance from supervisors. You might work for months without seeing any visible impact from, or without receiving feedback on, your work. Development is a slow process. Positive progress most often comes after the combined efforts of several Volunteers over the course of many years have had time to make their impact. Peace Corps expects and will aid you with developing the self-confidence, patience, and vision to continue working toward long-term goals without seeing immediate results. To overcome these difficulties, you will need maturity, flexibility, open-mindedness, resourcefulness, and a commitment to optimism.

Moldovans are warm, friendly, and hospitable, and the Peace Corps staff, your co-workers, and fellow Volunteers will support you during challenging times and congratulate on your successes. Judging by the experiences of former Volunteers, the rewards of service are well worth the difficulties encounterd. Overwhelmingly, Volunteers leave Moldova feeling that they have gained much more than they sacrificed during their service. If you are able to make the commitment to integrate into your community and work hard, you will be a successful Volunteer.

PEACE CORPS TRAINING

Overview of Pre-Service Training

Pre-service training begins the day you arrive in Moldova and ends when you are sworn in as a Volunteer (after week 8 for COD and ARBD Volunteers and week 10 for English Education and Health Education Volunteers). The days are full with plenty to accomplish and a great number of things to learn.

Peace Corps Moldova uses a community-based training approach. Trainees live in small villages with five or six other trainees from their project area. Language classes occur daily, and afternoons are usually devoted to self-directed activities and homework assignments. Once or twice a week, trainees come to a central hub site for technical, administrative, medical, safety, and joint cultural sessions and activities.

Due to the structure of Moldova's pre-service training program married couples may be required to live apart in different villages during training. Couples will see each other at the hub site on hub site days (twice a week) and are free to stay together with their respective host families on weekends and other times when the training schedule permits.

Assessment criteria, which you will be informed of early in pre-service training, will help you attain and demonstrate the necessary knowledge, skill, and attitudes (KSAs) for successful Volunteer service. A combination of staff, Volunteers and Moldovan partners worked to identify these KSAs and group them in competencies. The core competencies for all Volunteers in Moldova state that, for a Volunteer to successfully serve they will:

1) Commit to Peace Corps mission and professionalism;
2) Safely integrate into Moldovan society, and
3) Improve individual and organizational capacity.

During training, you will have periodic interviews with staff to discuss your progress toward attaining and demonstrating these competencies and, if helpful, be assisted with developing a plan of action for improvement.

The members of the training staff are Moldovan, and most of them have worked with Peace Corps for several years. They are a valuable resource for getting to know the Moldovan culture and language, and we expect that you will learn to use them for advice and support.

Technical Training
Technical training will prepare you to work in Moldova by building on the skills you already have and helping you develop new skills in a manner appropriate to the needs of the country. The Peace Corps staff, Moldova experts, and current Volunteers will conduct the training program. Training places great emphasis on learning how to transfer the skills you have to the community in which you will serve as a Volunteer.

Technical training will include sessions on the general economic and political environment in Moldova and strategies for working within such a framework. You will review your technical sector's goals and will meet with the Moldovan agencies and organizations that invited the Peace Corps to assist them. You will be supported and evaluated throughout the training to build the confidence and skills you need to undertake your project activities and be a productive member of your community.

Language Training
As a Peace Corps Volunteer, you will find that language skills are key to personal and professional satisfaction during your service. These skills are critical to your job performance, they help you integrate into your community, and they can ease your personal adaptation to the new surroundings. Therefore, language training is at the heart of the training program. You must successfully meet minimum language requirements to complete training and become a Volunteer. Moldovan language instructors teach formal language classes five days a week in small groups of four to five people.

Overwhelmingly trainees will study Romanian as their primary language. In addition, a limited number of Volunteers study Russian. The decision regarding who will study which language is a decision taken by staff and based upon the place you will likely be placed based upon the needs of specific site placements.

Your language training will incorporate a community-based approach. In addition to classroom time, you will be given assignments to work on outside of the classroom and with your host family. The goal is to get you to a point of basic social communication skills so you can practice and develop language skills further once you are at your site. Prior to being sworn in as a Volunteer, you will work on strategies to continue language studies during your service.

Cross-Cultural Training
As part of your pre-service training, you will live with a Moldovan host family. This experience is designed to ease your transition to life at your site. Families participate in an orientation conducted by Peace Corps staff to explain the purpose of pre-service training and to assist them in helping you adapt to living in Moldova. Many Volunteers form strong and lasting friendships with their host families.

Cross-cultural and community development training will help you improve your communication skills and understand your role as a facilitator of development. You will be exposed to topics such as community mobilization, conflict resolution, gender and development, nonformal and adult education strategies, and political structures. You will also have opportunities to take field trips to historic sites and to learn traditional songs and dances.

Health Training
During pre-service training, you will be given basic medical training and information. You will be expected to practice preventive health care and to take responsibility for your own health by adhering to all medical policies. Trainees are required to attend all medical sessions. The topics include preventive health measures and minor and major medical issues that you might encounter while in Moldova. Nutrition, mental health, setting up a safe living compound, and how to avoid HIV/AIDS and other sexually transmitted diseases (STDs) are also covered.

Safety Training
During the safety training sessions, you will learn how to adopt a lifestyle that reduces your risks at home, at work, and during your travels. You will also learn appropriate, effective strategies for coping with unwanted attention and about your individual responsibility for promoting safety throughout your service.

Additional Trainings During Volunteer Service

In its commitment to institutionalize quality training, the Peace Corps has implemented a training system that provides Volunteers with continual opportunities to examine their commitment to Peace Corps service while increasing their technical and cross-cultural skills. During service, there are usually three training events. The titles and objectives for those trainings are as follows:

- In-service training: *Provides an opportunity for Volunteers to upgrade their technical, language, and project development skills while sharing their experiences and reaffirming their commitment after having served for three to six months.*

- Midterm conference (done in conjunction with technical sector in-service): *Assists Volunteers in reviewing their first year, reassessing their personal and project objectives, and planning for their second year of service.*

- Close-of-service conference: *Prepares Volunteers for the future after Peace Corps service and reviews their respective projects and personal experiences.*

The number, length, and design of these trainings are adapted to country-specific needs and conditions. The key to the training system is that training events are integrated and interrelated, from the pre-departure orientation through the end of your service, and are planned, implemented, and evaluated cooperatively by the training staff, Peace Corps staff, and Volunteers.

YOUR HEALTH CARE AND SAFETY IN MOLDOVA

The Peace Corps' highest priority is maintaining the good health and safety of every Volunteer. Peace Corps medical programs emphasize the preventive, rather than the curative, approach to disease. The Peace Corps in Moldova maintains a clinic with a full-time medical officer, who takes care of Volunteers' primary health care needs. Additional medical services, such as testing and basic treatment, are also available in Moldova at local hospitals. If you become seriously ill, you will be transported either to an American-standard medical facility in the region or to the United States.

Health Issues in Moldova

Major health problems among Volunteers in Moldova are rare and must can be avoided by taking preventive measures to stay healthy. The most common health problems in Moldova also exist in the United States. These include colds, allergies, diarrhea, hemorrhoids, constipation, sinus infections, skin infections, headaches, dental problems, minor injuries, STDs, adjustment disorders, emotional problems, and alcohol abuse. These issues may be more frequent or compounded by life in Moldova because certain environmental factors here raise the risk of or exacerbate the severity of certain illnesses and injuries.

Under local law, foreign residents are required to have proof of a negative HIV/AIDS test to receive a residency permit. The law requires that the test be done in Moldova; any HIV test done in the States cannot be used. The first or second day after your arrival in Moldova, the Peace Corps medical officers will draw blood in collaboration with the local health department and send the blood for analysis anonymously. Copies of the negative results will be sent to the governmental agency responsible for issuing the residency permits.

Helping You Stay Healthy

The Peace Corps will provide you with all the necessary inoculations, medications, and information to stay healthy. Upon your arrival in Moldova, you will receive a medical handbook. At the end of training, you will receive a medical kit with supplies to take care of mild illnesses and first aid needs. The contents of the kit are listed later in this chapter.

During pre-service training, you will have access to basic medical supplies through the medical officer. However, you will be responsible for your own supply of prescription drugs and any other specific medical supplies you require, as the Peace Corps will not order these items during training. Please bring a three-month supply of any prescription drugs you use, since they may not be available here and it may take several months for shipments to arrive.

You will have physicals at midservice and at the end of your service. If you develop a serious medical problem during your service, the medical officer in Moldova will consult with the Office of Medical Services in Washington, D.C. If it is determined that your condition cannot be treated in Moldova, you may be sent out of the country for further evaluation and care.

Maintaining Your Health

As a Volunteer, you must accept considerable responsibility for your own health. Proper precautions will significantly reduce your risk of serious illness or injury. The adage "An ounce of prevention ..." becomes extremely important in areas where diagnostic and treatment facilities are not up to the standards of the United States. The most important of your responsibilities in Moldova is to take the following preventive measures:.Many illnesses that afflict Volunteers worldwide are entirely preventable if proper food and water precautions are taken. These illnesses include food poisoning, parasitic infections, hepatitis A, dysentery, Guinea worms, tapeworms, and typhoid fever. Your medical officer will discuss specific standards for water and food preparation in Moldova during pre-service training.

Abstinence is the only certain choice for preventing infection with HIV and other sexually transmitted diseases. You are taking risks if you choose to be sexually active. To lessen risk, use a condom every time you have sex. Whether your partner is a host country citizen, a fellow Volunteer, or anyone else, do not assume this person is free of HIV/AIDS or other STDs. You will receive more information from the medical officer about this important issue.

Volunteers are expected to adhere to an effective means of birth control to prevent an unplanned pregnancy. Your medical officer can help you decide on the most appropriate method to suit your individual needs. Contraceptive methods are available without charge from the medical officer.

It is critical to your health that you promptly report to the medical office or other designated facility for scheduled immunizations, and that you let the medical officer know immediately of significant illnesses and injuries.

Women's Health Information

Pregnancy is treated in the same manner as other Volunteer health conditions that require medical attention but also have programmatic ramifications. The Peace Corps is responsible for determining the medical risk and the availability of appropriate medical care if the Volunteer remains in-country. Given the circumstances under which Volunteers live and work in Peace Corps countries, it is rare that the Peace Corps' medical and programmatic standards for continued service during pregnancy can be met.

If feminine hygiene products are not available for you to purchase on the local market, the Peace Corps medical officer in Moldova will provide them. If you require a specific product, please bring a three-month supply with you.

Your Peace Corps Medical Kit

The Peace Corps medical officer will provide you with a kit that contains basic items necessary to prevent and treat illnesses that may occur during service. Kit items can be periodically restocked at the medical office.

Medical Kit Contents

Ace bandages

Adhesive tape

American Red Cross First Aid & Safety Handbook

Antacid tablets (Tums)

Antibiotic ointment (Bacitracin/Neomycin/Polymycin B)

Antiseptic antimicrobial skin cleaner (Hibiclens)

Band-Aids

Butterfly closures

Calamine lotion

Cepacol lozenges

Condoms

Dental floss

Diphenhydramine HCL 25 mg (Benadryl)

Insect repellent stick (Cutter's)

Iodine tablets (for water purification)

Lip balm (Chapstick)

Oral rehydration salts

Oral thermometer (Fahrenheit)

Pseudoephedrine HCL 30 mg (Sudafed)

Robitussin-DM lozenges (for cough)

Scissors

Sterile gauze pads
Tetrahydrozaline eyedrops (Visine)
Tinactin (antifungal cream)
Tweezers

Before You Leave: A Medical Checklist

If there has been any change in your health—physical, mental, or dental—since you submitted your examination reports to the Peace Corps, you must immediately notify the Office of Medical Services. Failure to disclose new illnesses, injuries, allergies, or pregnancy can endanger your health and may jeopardize your eligibility to serve.

If your dental exam was done more than a year ago, or if your physical exam is more than two years old, contact the Office of Medical Services to find out whether you need to update your records. If your dentist or Peace Corps dental consultant has recommended that you undergo dental treatment or repair, you must complete that work and make sure your dentist sends requested confirmation reports or X-rays to the Office of Medical Services.

If you wish to avoid having duplicate vaccinations, contact your physician's office to obtain a copy of your immunization record and bring it to your pre-departure orientation. If you have any immunizations prior to Peace Corps service, the Peace Corps cannot reimburse you for the cost. The Peace Corps will provide all the immunizations necessary for your overseas assignment, either at your pre-departure orientation or shortly after you arrive in Moldova. You do not need to begin taking malaria medication prior to departure.

Bring a three-month supply of any prescription or over-the-counter medication you use on a regular basis, including birth control pills. Although the Peace Corps cannot reimburse you for this three-month supply, it will order refills during your service. While awaiting shipment—which can take several months—you will be dependent on your own medication supply. The Peace Corps will not pay for herbal or nonprescribed medications, such as St. John's wort, glucosamine, selenium, or antioxidant supplements.

You are encouraged to bring copies of medical prescriptions signed by your physician. This is not a requirement, but they might come in handy if you are questioned in transit about carrying a three-month supply of prescription drugs.

If you wear eyeglasses, bring two pairs with you—a pair and a spare. If a pair breaks, the Peace Corps will replace them, using the information your doctor in the United States provided on the eyeglasses form during your examination. The Peace Corps discourages you from using contact lenses during your service to reduce your risk of developing a serious infection or other eye disease. Most Peace Corps countries do not have appropriate water and sanitation to support eye care with the use of contact lenses. The Peace Corps will not supply or replace contact lenses or associated solutions unless an ophthalmologist has recommended their use for a specific medical condition and the Peace Corps' Office of Medical Services has given approval.

If you are eligible for Medicare, are over 50 years of age, or have a health condition that may restrict your future participation in health care plans, you may wish to consult an insurance specialist about unique coverage needs before your departure. The Peace Corps will provide all necessary health care from the time you leave for your pre-departure orientation until you complete your service. When you finish, you will be entitled to the post-service health care benefits described in the Peace Corps *Volunteer Handbook*. You may wish to consider keeping an existing health plan in effect during your service if you think age or pre-existing conditions might prevent you from re-enrolling in your current plan when you return home.

Safety and Security—Our Partnership

Serving as a Volunteer overseas entails certain safety and security risks. Living and traveling in an unfamiliar environment, a limited understanding of the local language and culture, and the perception of being a wealthy American are some of the factors that can put a Volunteer at risk. Property theft and burglaries are not uncommon. Incidents of physical and sexual assault do occur, although almost all Volunteers complete their two years of service without serious personal safety problems.

Beyond knowing that Peace Corps approaches safety and security as a partnership with you, it might be helpful to see how this partnership works. Peace Corps has policies, procedures, and training in place to promote your safety. We depend on you to follow those policies and to put into practice what you have learned. An example of how this works in practice—in this case to help manage the risk of burglary—is:

- Peace Corps assesses the security environment where you will live and work
- Peace Corps inspects the house where you will live according to established security criteria
- Peace Corp provides you with resources to take measures such as installing new locks
- Peace Corps ensures you are welcomed by host country authorities in your new community
- Peace Corps responds to security concerns that you raise
- You lock your doors and windows
- You adopt a lifestyle appropriate to the community where you live
- You get to know neighbors
- You decide if purchasing personal articles insurance is appropriate for you
- You don't change residences before being authorized by Peace Corps
- You communicate concerns that you have to Peace Corps staff

This *Welcome Book* contains sections on: Living Conditions and Volunteer Lifestyle; Peace Corps Training; and Your Health Care and Safety that all include important safety and security information to help you understand this partnership. The Peace Corps makes every effort to give Volunteers the tools they need to function in the safest way possible, because working to maximize the safety and security of Volunteers is our highest priority. Not only do we provide you with training and tools to prepare for the unexpected, but we teach you to identify, reduce, and manage the risks you may encounter.

Factors that Contribute to Volunteer Risk
There are several factors that can heighten a Volunteer's risk, many of which are within the Volunteer's control. By far the most common crime that Volunteers experience is theft. Thefts often occur when Volunteers are away from their sites, in crowded locations (such as markets or on public transportation), and when leaving items unattended.

Before you depart for Moldova there are several measures you can take to reduce your risk:

- Leave valuable objects in U.S.
- Leave copies of important documents and account numbers with someone you trust in the U.S.
- Purchase a hidden money pouch or "dummy" wallet as a decoy
- Purchase personal articles insurance

After you arrive in Moldova, you will receive more detailed information about common crimes, factors that contribute to Volunteer risk, and local strategies to reduce that risk. For example, Volunteers in Moldova learn to:

- Choose safe routes and times for travel, and travel with someone trusted by the community whenever possible
- Make sure one's personal appearance is respectful of local customs
- Avoid high-crime areas
- Know the local language to get help in an emergency
- Make friends with local people who are respected in the community
- Limit alcohol consumption

As you can see from this list, you must be willing to work hard and adapt your lifestyle to minimize the potential for being a target for crime. As with anywhere in the world, crime does exist in Moldova. You can reduce your risk by avoiding situations that place you at risk and by taking precautions. Crime at the village or town level is less frequent than in the large cities; people know each other and generally are less likely to steal from their neighbors. Tourist attractions in large towns are favorite worksites for pickpockets.

While whistles and exclamations may be fairly common on the street, this behavior can be reduced if you dress conservatively, abide by local cultural norms, and respond according to the training you will receive.

Support from Staff

If a trainee or Volunteer is the victim of a safety incident, Peace Corps staff is prepared to provide support. All Peace Corps posts have procedures in place to respond to incidents of crime committed against Volunteers. The first priority for all posts in the aftermath of an incident is to ensure the Volunteer is safe and receiving medical treatment as needed. After assuring the safety of the Volunteer, Peace Corps staff response may include reassessing the Volunteer's worksite and housing arrangements and making any adjustments, as needed. In some cases, the nature of the incident may necessitate a site or housing transfer. Peace Corps staff will also assist Volunteers with preserving their rights to pursue legal sanctions against the perpetrators of the crime. It is very important that Volunteers report incidents as they occur, not only to protect their peer Volunteers, but also to preserve the future right to prosecute. Should Volunteers decide later in the process that they want to proceed with the prosecution of their assailant, this option may no longer exist if the evidence of the event has not been preserved at the time of the incident.

Staying Safe: Don't Be a Target for Crime

You must be prepared to take on a large degree of responsibility for your own safety. You can make yourself less of a target, ensure that your home is secure, and develop relationships in your community that will make you an unlikely victim of crime. While the factors that contribute to your risk in Moldova may be different, in many ways you can do what you would do if you moved to a new city anywhere: Be cautious, check things out, ask questions, learn about your neighborhood, know where the more risky locations are, use common sense, and be aware. You can reduce your vulnerability to crime by integrating into your community, learning the local language, acting responsibly, and abiding by Peace Corps policies and procedures. Serving safely and effectively in Moldova will require that you accept some restrictions on your current lifestyle.

Volunteers attract a lot of attention both in large cities and at their sites, but they are likely to receive more negative attention in highly populated centers than at their sites, where "family," friends, and colleagues look out for them. While whistles and exclamations are fairly common on the street, this behavior can be reduced if you dress conservatively, avoid eye contact, and do not respond to unwanted attention. In addition, keep your money out of sight by using an undergarment money pouch. Do not keep your money in the outside pockets of backpacks, in coat pockets, or in fanny packs. Always walk with a companion at night and avoid drawing unneeded attention by speaking loudly or obviously speaking English.

Most security incidents involving Peace Corps Volunteers in Moldova involve alcohol. These incidents also tend to occur when Volunteers gather in Chisinau or other large towns late at night, when their awareness may be lowered as a result of alcohol consumption. It is important that Volunteers recognize the danger of being in places where people are consuming (often overconsuming) alcohol and where a group of Volunteers may receive unwanted attention.

Crime Data for Moldova
Crime data and statistics for Ukraine, which is updated yearly, are available at the following link: http://www.peacecorps.gov/countrydata/moldova

Please take the time to review this important information

Few Peace Corps Volunteers are victims of serious crimes and crimes that do occur overseas are investigated and prosecuted by local authorities through the local courts system. If you are the victim of a crime, you will decide if you wish to pursue prosecution. If you decide to prosecute, Peace Corps will be there to assist you. One of our tasks is to ensure you are fully informed of your options and understand how the local legal process works. Peace Corps will help you ensure your rights are protected to the fullest extent possible under the laws of the country.

If you are the victim of a serious crime, you will learn how to get to a safe location as quickly as possible and contact your Peace Corps office. It's important that you notify Peace Corps as soon as you can so Peace Corps can provide you with the help you need.

Volunteer Safety Support in Moldova

The Peace Corps' approach to safety is a five-pronged plan to help you stay safe during your service and includes the following: information sharing, Volunteer training, site selection criteria, a detailed emergency action plan, and protocols for addressing safety and security incidents. Moldova's in-country safety program is outlined below.

The Peace Corps/Moldova office will keep you informed of any issues that may impact Volunteer safety through information sharing. Regular updates will be provided in Volunteer newsletters and in memorandums from the country director. In the event of a critical situation or emergency, you will be contacted through the emergency communication network. An important component of the capacity of Peace Corps to keep you informed is your buy-in to the partnership concept with the Peace Corps staff. It is expected that you will do your part in ensuring that Peace Corps staff members are kept apprised of your movements in-country so they are able to inform you.

Volunteer training will include sessions on specific safety and security issues in Moldova. This training will prepare you to adopt a culturally appropriate lifestyle and exercise judgment that promotes safety and reduces risk in your home, at work, and while traveling. Safety training is offered throughout service and is integrated into the language, cross-cultural aspects, health, and other components of training. You will be expected to successfully complete all training competencies in a variety of areas, including safety and security, as a condition of service.

Certain site selection criteria are used to determine safe housing for Volunteers before their arrival. The Peace Corps staff works closely with host communities and counterpart agencies to help prepare them for a Volunteer's arrival and to establish expectations of their respective roles in supporting the Volunteer. Each site is inspected before the Volunteer's arrival to ensure placement in appropriate, safe, and secure housing and worksites. Site selection is based, in part, on any relevant site history; access to medical, banking, postal, and other essential services; availability of communications, transportation, and markets; different housing options and living arrangements; and other Volunteer support needs.

You will also learn about Peace Corps/Moldova's detailed emergency action plan, which is implemented in the event of civil or political unrest or a natural disaster. When you arrive at your site, you will complete and submit a site locator form with your address, contact information, and a map to your house. If there is a security threat, you will gather with other Volunteers in Moldova at predetermined locations until the situation is resolved or the Peace Corps decides to evacuate.

Finally, in order for the Peace Corps to be fully responsive to the needs of Volunteers, it is imperative that Volunteers immediately report any security incident to the Peace Corps office. The Peace Corps has established protocols for addressing safety and security incidents in a timely and appropriate manner, and it collects and evaluates safety and security data to track trends and develop strategies to minimize risks to future Volunteers.

DIVERSITY AND CROSS-CULTURAL ISSUES

In fulfilling its mandate to share the face of America with host countries, the Peace Corps is making special efforts to assure that all of America's richness is reflected in the Volunteer corps. More Americans of color are serving in today's Peace Corps than at any time in recent history. Differences in race, ethnic background, age, religion, and sexual orientation are expected and welcomed among our Volunteers. Part of the Peace Corps' mission is to help dispel any notion that Americans are all of one origin or race and to establish that each of us is as thoroughly American as the other despite our many differences.

Our diversity helps us accomplish that goal. In other ways, however, it poses challenges. In Moldova, as in other Peace Corps host countries, Volunteers' behavior, lifestyle, background, and beliefs are judged in a cultural context very different from their own. Certain personal perspectives or characteristics commonly accepted in the United States may be quite uncommon, unacceptable, or even repressed in Moldova.

Outside of Moldova's capital, residents of rural communities have had relatively little direct exposure to other cultures, races, religions, and lifestyles. What people view as typical American behavior or norms may be a misconception, such as the belief that all Americans are rich and have blond hair and blue eyes. The people of Moldova are justly known for their generous hospitality to foreigners; however, members of the community in which you will live may display a range of reactions to cultural differences that you present.

To ease the transition and adapt to life in Moldova, you may need to make some temporary, yet fundamental compromises in how you present yourself as an American and as an individual. For example, female trainees and Volunteers may not be able to exercise the independence available to them in the United States; political discussions need to be handled with great care; and some of your personal beliefs may best remain undisclosed. You will need to develop techniques and personal strategies for coping with these and other limitations. The Peace Corps staff will lead diversity and sensitivity discussions during pre-service training and will be on call to provide support, but the challenge ultimately will be your own.

Overview of Diversity in Moldova

The Peace Corps staff in Moldova recognizes the adjustment issues that come with diversity and will endeavor to provide support and guidance. During pre-service training, several sessions will be held to discuss diversity and coping mechanisms. We look forward to having male and female Volunteers from a variety of races, ethnic groups, ages, religions, and sexual orientations, and hope that you will become part of a diverse group of Americans who take pride in supporting one another and demonstrating the richness of American culture.

What Might a Volunteer Face?

Possible Issues for Female Volunteers

Traditional or stereotyped gender roles are more prevalent in Moldova than they are in the United States. One estimate stated that Moldovan women do 300 percent more work in the home than men do. And it is common for a man to enter a room and shake every other man's hand while completely ignoring the women who are present. Although Americans are often bothered by such behavior, women do not have a subordinate role in Moldova. Historically, they have been a vital part of the workforce, taking on both managerial and supervisory positions. Moldovan women work as school administrators, business owners, doctors, local government officials, and members of Parliament.

Female Volunteers should not expect, however, to be able to continue all of their American practices in Moldova. Adapting to local mores and customs is a necessity for Peace Corps Volunteers wherever they are. Moldovan women generally lead more restricted lifestyles than American women do. For instance, Moldovan women do not go out alone at night, and jogging or walking alone for exercise is uncommon. Women in villages do not usually smoke in public, and all Moldovans tend to speak more quietly than Americans do in public places. While these activities are not forbidden for Volunteers, sometimes they have to make compromises and alter their behavior. Female Volunteers are advised to avoid eye contact with men who are strangers, especially on buses and in the street.

Volunteer Comment

"As a female Volunteer, expect to be kissed on the hand a lot, as hand kissing is a traditional greeting here in Moldova. You should also be prepared to answer repeated questions regarding your marital status. In my work, I have encountered situations where older men have considered me to have a diminished capacity for business or work because I am a woman. Despite this, I have managed to carry out many successful projects in my community and have enjoyed my time in Moldova."

Possible Issues for Volunteers of Color

African-American Volunteers often express frustration and disappointment at being asked where they are from because when they answer "African American" or "black American," some Moldovans react with surprise or disbelief. Although they may be the subject of frequent stares and questions as well as occasional insults, most African-American Volunteers say they are well accepted in their communities after an initial settling-in period. There is a small population of students and businesspeople from Africa in Chisinau, and some African Americans are assigned to the U.S. Embassy.

Hispanic American Volunteers have found that some Moldovans stereotype them as similar to the characters they watch in the popular Latin American soap operas on television. Also, some Hispanic American Volunteers have been misidentified as Romany (a.k.a., gypsies) and have been harassed according to local stereotypes and prejudices related to this population.

Asian-American Volunteers often find that they stand out more than Caucasians, as there are relatively few "East Asians" (Japanese, Chinese,

Southeast Asians) in Moldova. People may assume that Asian-American Volunteers are from China, and may express skepticism that they are Americans. In addition some Asian American Volunteers have reported being stopped more frequently by local police to check their identification. While much of this extra attention is not intended to be negative, it can be tiresome. Many of these irritations dissipate as Volunteers become better known in their communities.

Volunteer Comments

"As an African American, I found the responses to me annoying and frustrating the first few months, but I invented my own ways of survival and won my way into people's warm hearts. I was quietly assertive, outgoing and determined to talk about diversity and my Afro-African American heritage. My experience in Chisinau was different than when I lived in the village during training, and having some diversity in Chisinau did make a difference. My advice is to be positive, educate the people and let them know that everyone deserves a chance no matter the color of their skin."

"As a Native American serving in Moldova, I found it to be rather disheartening at first. Because I am darker in complexion than Moldovans, I was often called racial names, which bothered me greatly at first. I am also pierced in several visible places (eyebrow, lip, and ears) and am constantly being stared at and talked about. However, with a little education, for both myself and Moldovans, I found these behaviors to decrease over time. They can be tiresome and irritating, but in the end the benefits outweigh the temporary discomforts."

Possible Issues for Senior Volunteers
Respect comes with age in Moldova. Younger Volunteers may have to work harder than their older colleagues to be accepted as professionals. It is not uncommon for younger Volunteers to look to older Volunteers for advice and support. Some seniors find this a very enjoyable part of their Volunteer experience, while others choose not to fill this role. Overall, senior Volunteers are highly valued for the wealth of experience they bring to their communities and counterparts.

Volunteer Comments

"At this time of your life, you have much to offer Moldovans, more in many ways than the younger Volunteers. You know business in depth, you know life in depth, and you can be a solid, steadying influence in the Peace Corps and in Moldova. Saying that this is the 'Toughest Job You'll Ever Love' is not just a quaint, patriotic slogan; it's true—perhaps even more so at our age. You no longer fear life, and you have good, practical, and tried ideas."

"Do not worry about being older than many or most of the other Volunteers. From the first day, you will see that Peace Corps Volunteers are as wise, caring, hardworking, generous, tolerant, and fun to be with as we seniors believe we are. If you sometimes lead, sometimes follow, and are always willing to participate at some level, you will be effective and enriched. As an older Volunteer in Moldova (I'm 70), I know that, while I may have added years to my life while being in the Peace Corps, I have truly added life to my years!"

Possible Issues for Gay, Lesbian, or Bisexual Volunteers
Homosexuality is misunderstood and generally not accepted by the majority of Moldovans, and discussing the issue of sexual orientation may be problematic. It is advisable to use discretion because you may experience difficulties if your community becomes aware of your sexual orientation, compromising your ability to be effective. Peace Corps staff in Moldova can provide you with information on organizations in Moldova that are working on issues concerning sexual orientation, and there is a Volunteer Gender Workgroup of gay, lesbian, bisexual and supportive straight Volunteers, whose coordinator and members can also provide information and support. You may also find helpful information on serving in the Peace Corps as a gay or lesbian from a group of returned Volunteers affiliated with the National Peace Corps Association (for more information, go to www.lgbrpcv.org; for country-specific info, go to www.gay.md).

Gay and lesbian Volunteers can (and do) productively serve and have positive experiences here in Moldova. However, there are some issues you will face in Moldova that may be quite different from what you were used to in the States. There is a small community of gay, lesbian and bisexual Moldovans in Chisinau, which is becoming increasingly active and hosts social events, but there are few other social activities or meeting places. As a result, many gays and lesbians experience feelings of loneliness and isolation. This is especially true for those who choose closeted lives in communities outside of Chisinau. As a result, you will encounter bias and prejudice about gays and lesbians. You will need to be cautious about who you come out to amongst your Moldovan friends. However, you are encouraged to be out with Peace Corps Staff and Volunteers to lessen the feeling of isolation. Peace Corps Moldova is committed to ensuring an environment that is safe, secure, and accepting of all forms of diversity, and gays, lesbians and bisexuals should feel comfortable talking about whatever issues they are facing. You will find staff and your Volunteer peers to be very supportive.

Volunteer Comment

"Moldova is no different from other Peace Corps countries in that homosexuality is feared, judged, and misunderstood. There is pressure on everyone here to get married and have children. I recommend extreme caution in choosing whom you come out to. On the other hand, the other Volunteers are very supportive, and a small but friendly gay, lesbian, and bisexual community exists in Chisinau."

Possible Religious Issues for Volunteers

There are no official or societal restrictions with regard to religious belief in Moldova. The primary religion is Eastern Orthodox Christianity, which is divided between those affiliated with the Romanian Orthodox Church and those affiliated with the Russian Orthodox Church. There are also congregations of Jews, Roman Catholics, Baptists, Seventh-Day Adventists, Mormons, and others. Religion is an important part of life for many, but by no means all, Moldovans. Most towns and villages have at least one Orthodox church, and some also have small Baptist churches.

Volunteer Comments

"The Romanian Orthodox Church does not recognize Roman Catholics as communicants, so full participation in services here can be difficult. There are not many Roman Catholic churches in Moldova, and they will most likely not be close to your site. You may wish to bring books or other materials to help you maintain your spiritual practices when attending church is not possible. However, a positive side of this for me has been that when I can join in on the Eucharist, I am often more grateful and attentive than when I took its availability for granted."

"As a Jew in Moldova, I have been open in my Jewish observance. I pray every morning and have a religiously restricted diet. Both of my host families were aware of this and were accommodating, though rather perplexed. If there is a religious event that I am uncomfortable attending, I just plan ahead and make an excuse to avoid it. There is a small, but active Jewish community in Chisinau, and I have attended holiday, Sabbath, and daily services there. Unfortunately, many other activities are scheduled on Saturdays, which has often made participating in services difficult."

"As a Mormon, I find a great amount of curiosity from the community I live in. Exposing yourself to religious experiences in Moldova isn't hard, but be aware that church attendance by those with faiths other than Eastern Orthodox is difficult. At times, you may feel like the only Mormon, Catholic, Jew, etc. in the whole country. It is not impossible to meet people of your own faith, however. For example, I can take an hour's bus ride on Sunday to meet with other Mormons. Most Moldovans don't know about the vast number of different religious denominations in the United States, so discussing one another's religious beliefs is a great way to exchange ideas and culture."

Possible Issues for Volunteers With Disabilities
As part of the medical clearance process, the Peace Corps Office of Medical Services determined that you were physically and emotionally capable, with or without reasonable accommodations, to perform a full tour of Volunteer service in Moldova without unreasonable risk of harm to yourself or interruption of service. The Peace Corps/Moldova staff will work with disabled Volunteers to make reasonable accommodations for them in training, housing, jobsites, or other areas to enable them to serve safely and effectively.

As a disabled Volunteer in Moldova, you may find that you face a special set of challenges. In Moldova, as in other parts of the world, some people may hold prejudicial attitudes about individuals with disabilities and may discriminate against them. In addition, there is little of the infrastructure to accommodate individuals with disabilities that has been developed in the United States.

Nonetheless, as part of the medical clearance process, the Peace Corps Office of Medical Services determined that you were physically and emotionally capable, with or without reasonable accommodations, of serving in Moldova without unreasonable risk of harm to yourself or interruption of your service. The Peace Corps Moldova staff will work with disabled Volunteers to make reasonable accommodations for them in training, housing, job sites, or other areas to enable them to serve safely and effectively.

Possible Issues for Married Volunteers
Married couples who are in different programs may have to live with separate host families in separate villages throughout PST. This is due to the fact that each site contains Trainees from only one program. It may be impossible to find housing near the location of two program sites or within daily commuting distance. The spouses see each other on hub site days, and may travel to visit each other on weekends and other times allowed by the training schedule.

FREQUENTLY ASKED QUESTIONS

How much luggage am I allowed to bring to Moldova?
Most airlines have baggage size and weight limits and assess charges for transport of baggage that exceeds those limits. The Peace Corps has its own size and weight limits and will not pay the cost of transport for baggage that exceeds these limits. The Peace Corps' allowance is two checked pieces of luggage with combined dimensions of both pieces not to exceed 107 inches (length + width + height) and a carry-on bag with dimensions of no more than 45 inches. Checked baggage should not exceed 100 pounds total with a maximum weight of 50 pounds for any one bag.

Peace Corps Volunteers are not allowed to take pets, weapons, explosives, radio transmitters (shortwave radios are permitted), automobiles, or motorcycles to their overseas assignments. Do not pack flammable materials or liquids such as lighter fluid, cleaning solvents, hair spray, or aerosol containers. This is an important safety precaution.

What is the electric current in Moldova?
The current in Moldova is 220 volts. If you bring American electronics (which generally run on 110 volts) with you, you will need both a transformer to convert the 110 volts into 220 volts and a converter to fit the

American-style plug into a Moldovan outlet. Transformers come in varying wattages, but they are designed to be used primarily with blow dryers, irons, and the like; they are not designed for more sensitive equipment like laptops and cameras (many of which can support 220 volts., but you should always be cetain before plugging them in).

How much money should I bring?

Volunteers are expected to live at the same level as the people in their community. You will be given a settling-in allowance and a monthly living allowance, which should cover your expenses. Volunteers often wish to bring additional money for vacation travel to other countries. Credit cards and traveler's checks are preferable to cash. If you choose to bring extra money, bring the amount that will suit your own travel plans and needs.

When can I take vacation and have people visit me?

Each Volunteer accrues two vacation days per month of service (excluding training). Leave may not be taken during training, the first three months of service, or the last three months of service, except in conjunction with an authorized emergency leave. Family and friends are welcome to visit you after pre-service training and the first three months of service as long as their stay does not interfere with your work. Extended stays at your site are not encouraged and may require permission from your country director. The Peace Corps is not able to provide your visitors with visa, medical, or travel assistance.

Will my belongings be covered by insurance?

The Peace Corps does not provide insurance coverage for personal effects; Volunteers are ultimately responsible for the safekeeping of their personal belongings. However, you can purchase personal property insurance before you leave. If you wish, you may contact your own insurance company; additionally, insurance application forms will be provided, and we encourage you to consider them carefully. Volunteers should not ship or take valuable items overseas. Jewelry, watches, radios, cameras, and expensive appliances are subject to loss, theft, and breakage, and in many places, satisfactory maintenance and repair services are not available.

Do I need an international driver's license?

Volunteers in Moldova do not need an international driver's license because they are prohibited from operating privately owned motorized vehicles. Most urban travel is by bus or taxi. Rural travel ranges from buses and minibuses to trucks, bicycles, and lots of walking. On very rare occasions, a Volunteer may be asked to drive a sponsor's vehicle, but this can occur only with prior written permission from the country director. Should this occur, the Volunteer may obtain a local driver's license. A U.S. driver's license will facilitate the process, so bring it with you just in case.

What should I bring as gifts for Moldovan friends and my host family?
This is not a requirement. A token of friendship is sufficient. Some gift suggestions include knickknacks for the house; pictures, books, or calendars of American scenes; souvenirs from your area; hard candies that will not melt or spoil; or photos to give away.

Where will my site assignment be when I finish training and how isolated will I be?
Peace Corps trainees are not assigned to individual sites until after they have completed pre-service training. This gives Peace Corps staff the opportunity to assess each trainee's technical and language skills prior to assigning sites, in addition to finalizing site selections with their ministry counterparts. If feasible, you may have the opportunity to provide input on your site preferences, including geographical location, distance from other Volunteers, and living conditions. However, keep in mind that many factors influence the site selection process and that the Peace Corps cannot guarantee placement where you would ideally like to be. Most Volunteers live in small towns or in rural villages and are usually within one hour from another Volunteer. Some sites require a 10- to 12-hour drive from the capital. There is at least one Volunteer based in each of the regional capitals and about five to eight Volunteers in the capital city.

How can my family contact me in an emergency?
The Peace Corps' Office of Special Services provides assistance in handling emergencies affecting trainees and Volunteers or their families. Before leaving the United States, instruct your family to notify the Office of Special Services immediately if an emergency arises, such as a serious illness or death of a family member. During normal business hours, the number for the Office of Special Services is 800.424.8580; select option 2, then extension 1470. After normal business hours and on weekends and holidays, the Special Services duty officer can be reached at the above number. For non-emergency questions, your family can get information from your country desk staff at the Peace Corps by calling 800.424.8580.

Can I call home from Moldova?

The cost of international calls can be high. American calling cards will not work in Moldova, but international phone cards can be purchased that will give you enough time to give your family your phone number and instructions on when to call you back. Moldova CyberCommunity calling cards for calling the United States from Moldova are readily available at kiosks in Chisinau for a reasonable price. If your home does not have a phone, you should be able to use a neighbor's phone or the local telephone office. International lines are clearest early in the mornings and on weekends. Moldovan time is seven hours ahead of Eastern Standard Time.

Should I bring a cellular phone with me?

Moldova has cellular phone service that covers most of the country. Peace Corps staff members carry cell phones to attend to emergency calls, and Volunteers are required to have cell phone as well. However, differences in technology make most U.S. cell phones incompatible with the Moldovan cellular phone network. Although the Moldovan cell network uses GSM technology, most GSM phones bought in the U.S. typically need to be "unlocked" before they will work here. These phones can be bought in the U.S., usually as world-band phones as well as on eBay. Volunteers are provided funds at the end of training to purchase a cell phone and receive funds for communication as part of their monthly allowances.

Will there be email and Internet access? Should I bring my computer?

There are a number of Internet service providers in Moldova and Volunteers are increasingly connected to the Internet at their permanent sites. An increasing number of Moldovan communities have high-speed Internet connectivity available. Some Volunteers remark how strange it is to have DSL in a home without gas or running water.

Volunteers who come to post with laptops generally report that they are glad that they did. Most laptops sold recently are able to handle both 110 and 220 volt (please be certain BEFORE actually inserting the plug in an outlet) power supplies although you may need an adapter for your plug. Bring a good carrying case for lugging your computer around. It is a good idea to check your warranty to see what options are available in Europe for any needed repairs. Load your software on your computer before you leave and bring only the manuals and disks you believe will be critical to have in Moldova. It is also a good idea to insure your computer.

WELCOME LETTERS FROM MOLDOVA VOLUNTEERS

Greetings and welcome to Moldova! My name is Selby Stebbins. As a health Volunteer, I'm assigned to both a school and a community health organization. During pre-service training, I didn't want to be a health education teacher in a grammar school. I only wanted to work at the community organization. However, as preparation for working in schools, we had a two-week "practice school" with children in our training village. To my surprise, I fell in love with teaching after the first class. A year later, it is one of the most rewarding things I do here. I also work with a group of peer educators at the school and have really enjoyed helping them put on after-school, health-related activities for their classmates.

Health education classes are taught in Romanian. I thought it would be impossible to learn enough Romanian in 10 weeks of training. Have faith! The language program here in Moldova is excellent, and you'll be proud of yourself, just as I was, when at the end of the first day of school you realize you just successfully taught several classes in a language other than English. The best advice I've received regarding coping with life in a foreign country is: "Be patient. The more patient you are with yourself and others, the more you will enjoy your experience." I have found this to be very true. Some days are more difficult than others, but when I have a rough moment, I try to remind myself that things in the United States didn't always go my way either. I don't regret one moment—difficult or humorous or just plain crazy—that I have spent here. The Peace Corps does many things to help Volunteers have a successful two years, but ultimately the quality of your experience rests upon your own willingness to work, to adapt, and to forgive yourself and others. Keep your heart and mind open for an incredible two years and that's what you will receive!

Here are a few things I am really glad I brought or had sent: a one-month supply of underwear, colored markers, a sun shower, lots of quality long underwear and gloves (in different weights, for winter), a waterproof jacket, waterproof boots, and good facial care products.

Things I wish I had brought (and now can't really get) include my professional books related to NGO development and health. I recommend that trainees send professional books by surface mail before they leave the United States. The books will not take up luggage space and will arrive by the time you need them.

Things I wish I had done before leaving include gathering materials related to my assignment. I wish I had visited local health organizations, the

American Cancer Society, the Red Cross, and so on in pursuit of posters, toothbrushes, pamphlets, medical diagrams, and more.

—Selby Stebbins

Today I have three sweet potatoes sitting in my living room and 75 kilograms of sand in two bags sitting outside my door. It is late, but I will do my best to get some seed potatoes out of those gifts from the United States. The other day it was pouring down rain and I was in back of a farm truck loaded with workers going to pick peppers and tomatoes. The workers laughed at how slow I was and asked how my back felt. It ached. We picked 33 sacks of peppers and about 50 crates of tomatoes.

It is seven kilometers to the fields, and the 15-year-old son of one of the farmers and I go out together and loaded down our bikes with vegetables to bring back. I don't mind the exercise. I go sometimes with my counterparts at work when they measure the growth patterns of our crops. We measure the leaves, count them, and then measure the height of the plant itself. When we harvested the sweet corn last week for sale in Chisinau, I wanted to go too just to make sure the corn was good; I even wanted to taste it before our first sale.

What I am trying to say is that life in Moldova is just life in general. It is hard and frustrating, and it is a challenge to try to figure out. Maybe the reason I like it here is that I want to drink in the whole experience, to immerse myself in Moldovans' lives, to feel their problems, and to revel in a success or two. I will always be the American. There is something different about me that I don't even recognize, but the community likes me working next to them and sharing their life experiences. I like listening and think I am learning more about what life is all about than I ever did back home.

—John Goodrick

I want to wish you all good luck! Training is long and arduous, but I believe in you all. Keep a positive outlook; enjoy the newness of the culture and the beginning of a great experience. When you think you can't do it anymore—around week seven of pre-service training—remember that it only gets better and others have survived it, too! So welcome to Moldova. It is a great place to work, and you will see the progress happening right in front of your eyes.

—Angie Carr

PACKING LIST

This list has been compiled by Volunteers serving in Moldova and is based on their experience. Use it as an informal guide in making your own list, bearing in mind that each experience is individual. There is no perfect list! You obviously cannot bring everything on the list, so consider those items that make the most sense to you personally and professionally. You can always have things sent to you later. As you decide what to bring, keep in mind that you have an 80-pound weight limit on baggage. And remember, you can get almost everything you need in Moldova.

General Clothing

Bring clothes that are comfortable, that can be mixed and matched, and that are easy to wash by hand (i.e., made of synthetics like polyester or acrylic). Dry cleaning is available but not reliable or inexpensive, and generally not available in villages. Moldovans place great emphasis on clothing and dressing neatly, including making sure clothes are ironed, so "permanent press" clothes are useful. Although most clothes are available locally, women who wear larger sizes may have difficulty finding those sizes in Moldova. Some specific suggestions follow.

- A variety of professional clothes for work (see earlier section titled Professionalism, Dress, and Behavior), i.e., Dockers-type pants and dress shirts and ties for men, and skirts and dresses for women.
- One or two dressy outfits for special events, such as a suit or blazer(s)/sports coat(s) for men.
- Two pairs of jeans.
- Pullover sweaters and cardigans (wool is best).
- One or two pairs of long shorts (short shorts are not appropriate).
- Swimsuit.
- Sweatsuit for relaxing at home.
- One all-weather coat for spring and fall and one <u>very</u> warm winter coat (e.g., down).
- Warm winter hat, earmuffs, and gloves or mittens.
- Socks, both wool and cotton. Dark colors work best—black and brown.

- Underwear (cotton for warm weather, thermal or silk for cold weather).
- Two or more sets of long underwear for winter (Volunteers recommend Duofold and Patagonia brands and items made of Capilene, polypropylene, silk, and a silk and wool blend).
- Pantyhose and tights for women (available in Moldova but quality may be poor).

Shoes

- Dress shoes for work; select comfortable styles.
- Sneakers, sandals, or other shoes that are easy to slip on and off.
- Two pairs of sturdy boots, one waterproof (e.g., rubber duck boots with removable lining) and the other warm and preferably dressier. Simple rubber boots can be bought here cheaply. The dressier boots can substitute for work shoes in winter.

Personal Hygiene and Toiletry Items

- Three-month supply of toiletries, as it may be difficult to find time to shop during training.
- Three-month supply of sanitary pads or tampons, if you require a particular brand (Tampax and local brands are available in Moldova).

Kitchen

- Basic cookbook, with measurement conversions and suggested substitutions.
- Plastic food storage bags.
- Measuring cups.
- Spices (some that are popular with Americans may be hard to find locally); popular items to bring include taco seasoning and ranch dip).

Miscellaneous

- Map of Eastern Europe.
- Musical instrument (if you play).
- Music and movies.
- Power converter for electrical appliances requiring them.
- Sewing kit.
- Small tool kit (a leatherman or Swiss Army knife may suffice).

- Teachers should bring a good set of markers and some "sharpies."
- Nail care items such as clippers and emery boards.
- Inexpensive, durable, water-resistant watch (replacement batteries are available here).
- Sleeping bag with stuff sack for traveling in cold weather (or it can be borrowed, although some Volunteers find the sleeping bag valuable for warmth in the winter).
- Laundry bag.
- Camera (35 mm compacts are best for travel). Note that Advantix film is not available and cannot be developed in Moldova and that processing of black-and-white film is not reliable. You can print digital photos in most large towns.
- Rechargeable battery set (that takes up to 220 volts).
- Money belt or pouch .
- Internal frame backpack.
- Small overnight bag.
- Envelopes of various sizes and U.S. postage stamps.
- Duct tape.
- Swiss army knife or Leatherman tool
- Set of towels (bath, hand, and face) – can be bought here, but quality is uncertain.
- Photos from home (postcards are good).
- Posters, picture frames, etc. to make your room homey.
- Bandannas and handkerchiefs.
- Frisbee.
- Games (e.g., Uno, Scrabble, Trivial Pursuit, chess, volleyball, etc.)

PRE-DEPARTURE CHECKLIST

The following list consists of suggestions for you to consider as you prepare to live outside the United States for two years. Not all items will be relevant to everyone, and the list does not include everything you should make arrangements for.

Family

- Notify family that they can call the Peace Corps' Office of Special Services at any time if there is a critical illness or death of a family member (24-hour telephone number: 800.424.8580, extension 1470).

- Give the Peace Corps' *On the Home Front* handbook to family and friends.

Passport/Travel

- Forward to the Peace Corps travel office all paperwork for the Peace Corps passport and visas.

- Verify that your luggage meets the size and weight limits for international travel.

- Obtain a personal passport if you plan to travel after your service ends. (Your Peace Corps passport will expire three months after you finish your service, so if you plan to travel longer, you will need a regular passport.)

Medical/Health

- Complete any needed dental and medical work.

- If you wear glasses, bring two pairs.

- Arrange to bring a three-month supply of all medications (including birth control pills) you are currently taking.

Insurance

- Make arrangements to maintain life insurance coverage.

- Arrange to maintain supplemental health coverage while you are away. (Even though the Peace Corps is responsible for your health care during Peace Corps service overseas, it is advisable for people who have pre-existing conditions to arrange for the continuation of their supplemental health coverage. If there is a lapse in coverage, it is often difficult and expensive to be reinstated.)

- Arrange to continue Medicare coverage if applicable.

Personal Papers
- Bring a copy of your certificate of marriage or divorce.

Voting
- Register to vote in the state of your home of record. (Many state universities consider voting and payment of state taxes as evidence of residence in that state.)

- Obtain a voter registration card and take it with you overseas.

- Arrange to have an absentee ballot forwarded to you overseas.

Personal Effects
- Purchase personal property insurance to extend from the time you leave your home for service overseas until the time you complete your service and return to the United States.

Financial Management
- Keep a bank account in your name in the U.S.

- Obtain student loan deferment forms from the lender or loan service.

- Execute a Power of Attorney for the management of your property and business.

- Arrange for deductions from your readjustment allowance to pay alimony, child support, and other debts through the Office of Volunteer Financial Operations at 800.424.8580, extension 1770.

- Place all important papers—mortgages, deeds, stocks, and bonds—in a safe deposit box or with an attorney or other caretaker.

CONTACTING PEACE CORPS HEADQUARTERS

This list of numbers will help connect you with the appropriate office at Peace Corps headquarters to answer various questions. You can use the toll-free number and extension or dial directly using the local numbers provided. Be sure to leave the toll-free number and extensions with your family so they can contact you in the event of an emergency.

Peace Corps Headquarters
Toll-free Number: 800.424.8580, Press 2, and then Ext. # (see below)

Peace Corps' Mailing Address: Peace Corps
Paul D. Coverdell Peace Corps Headquarters
1111 20th Street, NW
Washington, DC 20526

For Questions About:	Staff	Toll-free Extension	Direct/ Local Number
Responding to an Invitation	Office of Placement	Ext. 1840	202.692.1840
Programming or Country Information	Desk Officer Email: Moldova@peacecorps.gov	Ext. 2413	202.692.2422

For Questions About:	Staff	Toll-free Extension	Direct/ Local Number
Plane Tickets, Passports, Visas, or Other Travel Matters	Travel Officer (Sato Travel)	Ext. 1170	202.692.1170
Legal Clearance	Office of Placement	Ext. 1845	202.692.1845
Medical Clearance and Forms Processing (including dental)	Screening Nurse	Ext. 1500	202.692.1500
Medical Reimbursements	Handled by a Subcontractor		800.818.8772
Loan Deferments, Taxes, Readjustment Allowance Withdrawals, Power of Attorney	Volunteer Financial Operations	Ext. 1770	202.692.1770
Staging (Pre-departure Orientation) and Reporting Instructions	Office of Staging	Ext. 1865	202.692.1865

Note: You will receive comprehensive information (hotel and flight arrangements) three to five weeks before departure. This information is not available sooner.

Family Emergencies (to get information to a Volunteer overseas)	Office of Special Services	Ext. 1470 *(24 hours)*	202.692.1470

Made in the USA
Lexington, KY
03 March 2015